TABLE OF CONTENT

TABLE OF CONTENT 2

1. BLACKBERRY SOUFFLE RECIPE...4

2. LEMON BLUEBERRY CUP OFCAKES 5

3. BLUEBERRY NO-BAKE CHEESECAKE 6

4. CAPPUCCINO MOUSSE..7

5. CARAMEL PECAN PIE 8

6. CARROT CAKE CUP OFCAKES..9

7. CHOCOLATE CHERRY CAKE ROLL 10

8. CHOCOLATE-ORANGE BREAD PUDDING 13

9. CHOCOLATE TORTE 14

10. CINNAMON BREAD PUDDING 16

11. COCONUT CREAM PIE RECIPE 17

12. COCONUT MILKSHAKE 18

13. CREAM CHEESE POUND CAKE 19

14. DARK CHOCOLATE COFFEE CUP OFCAKES...21

15. GERMAN CHOCOLATE CAKE BARS...22

16. GINGERBREAD SOUFFLÉS 23

17. LEMON MERINGUE ICE CREAM 24

18. MINI BREAD PUDDINGS 25

19. MINI KEY LIME PIES 26

20. BUTTER CAKE..27

21. NO-BAKE CHOCOLATE SWIRL CHEESECAKE 29

22. NO BAKE LEMON TART 30

23. PEVERY CUSTARD TART 31

24. OLD-FASHIONED FRESH PEVERY ICE CREAM...32

25. PEANUT BUTTER PIE 34

26. POMEGRANATE PANNA COTTA 35

27. SUGARED PECAN PUMPKIN ICE CREAM 36

28. RASPBERRY-ALMOND CLAFOUTI 38

29. CHOCOLATE RASPBERRY SOUFLES...39

30. LEMON RASPBERRY CHEESECAKE BARS 40

31. PEVERY RASPBERRY COBBLER 42

32. SANGRIA JELLO SHOTS 43

33. STRAWBERRY CHEESECAKE 44

34. STRAWBERRY SORBET 46

35. STICKY GINGER CAKE WITH MASCARPONE AND GINGER CREAM RECIPE 46

36. SWEET POTATO CRÈME BRÛLÉE 48

37. TIRAMISU 49

1. BLACKBERRY SOUFFLE RECIPE

Prep Time 20 mins

Cook Time 12 mins

Total Time 32 mins

Ingredients

- 200g fresh blackberries
- 1 tbsp cornflour
- 2 tbsp patxaran liqueur or any blackberry liqueur
- 2 large egg whites
- 75g caster sugar
- Icing sugar for dusting
- Softened butter to grease the ramekins
- Extra caster sugar to coat the ramekins

Method

1. Set the oven to Gas Mark 5, 190 C, or 375 F.
2. With the aid of a pastry brush and the softened butter, grease 4 ramekins, taking care to brush the sides of the ramekins toward the outside to ensure they are thoroughly coated with the butter. Caster sugar should be used to coat the ramekins. Tap off any extra sugar. To set, put the ramekins in the refrigerator.
3. The blackberries should be heated slowly for 5 minutes, or until they are mushy. Mix the cornflour, liqueur, and some blackberry puree in a small cup of. Stir thoroughly. The blackberries in the pan can now have the cornflour mixture added to them. Stir over low heat until thick. After putting the mixture through a sieve, let it cool. Add the sugar gradually while continuing to whisk the egg whites until they are stiff and glossy.
4. Gently fold the remaining meringue into the cool blackberry puree after adding one large spoonful, being careful not to overmix.

5. With the aid of a palette knife, level the tops of the ramekins after spooning the mixture into them, tapping the bottoms to remove any air bubbles. To balance out the sides and give the ramekin an even rise, run your finger along the top edge.

6. Serve right away after baking for 12 minutes, or when the bread is well-risen.

2. LEMON BLUEBERRY CUP OFCAKES

Prep Time: 20 minutes

Cook Time: 20 minutes

Total Time: 2 hours, 40 minutes

Ingredients

- 1 and 1/2 cups of (188g) all-purpose flour (spoon & leveled)
- 2 tsp baking powder
- 1/2 tsp salt
- 1/2 cup of (115g) unsalted butter, softened to room temperature
- 1 cup of (200g) granulated sugar
- 1 Tbsp lemon zest (about 3 lemons)
- 2 large eggs, at room temperature
- 1 and 1/2 tsp pure vanilla extract
- 1/2 cup of (120ml) whole milk or buttermilk, at room temperature
- 1/4 cup of (60ml) lemon juice (about 2 lemons)
- 1 cup of (115g) fresh or refrigerated blueberries, tossed in 1 Tbsp flour
- Cream Cheese Frosting
- 8 oz (224g) full-fat block cream cheese, softened to room temperature
- 1/4 cup of (60g) unsalted butter, softened to room temperature
- 2 cups of (240g) confectioners' sugar

- 1 tsp pure vanilla extract
- pinch salt
- non-compulsory: lemon slices and extra blueberries for garnish

Instructions

1. Set the oven's temperature to 350°F (177°C). Make sure to use cup ofcake liners in a 12-cup of muffin tin. Since this recipe makes around 15 cup ofcakes, you'll have extras.
2. creating the batter In a sizable basin, mix the salt, baking soda, and flour. Place aside.
3. In a large bowl, whip the butter, sugar, and lemon zest for about 2 minutes on medium-high speed using a hand-held or stand mixer with a paddle attachment. As necessary, scrape the bowl's bottom and sides. Then, for about a minute, beat on medium-high speed while incorporating the eggs and vanilla essence. As necessary, scrape the bowl's bottom and sides. Turn the mixer to low speed, add the dry ingredients, and then gently add the milk and lemon juice. Just merge after beating. Add the floured blueberries after blending. Avoid overmixing.
4. To prevent spilling over the sides, only fill the liners 2/3 full as you pour or spoon the batter into them. When a toothpick put in the center of the cake comes out clean, bake for 18 to 21 minutes. Bake small cup ofcakes for around 30-36 minutes at the same oven temperature. Before icing, let the cup ofcakes cool fully.
5. Creating the icing Cream the butter and cream cheese in a large bowl for 2 minutes on medium speed with a hand-held or stand mixer equipped with a whisk or paddle attachment. Confectioners' sugar, vanilla extract, and salt should be added. After 30 seconds of low speed mixing, increase the speed to medium-high and beat for 2 minutes. If desired, add an additional pinch of salt after tasting. You should chill this frosting for at least 20 minutes before using it to create elaborate designs.
6. Once cup ofcakes have cooled, frost them and add a garnish if you choose. The cup ofcakes in the picture were piped using an Ateco #808 tip. Another option is to use a tiny icing spatula. Before serving, place decorated cup ofcakes in the refrigerator, uncovered, for at least 20 minutes to help the frosting set.
7. Cup ofcake leftovers can be covered and kept in the fridge for up to 5 days. Using a cup ofcake carrier makes transporting and storing them simple.

3. BLUEBERRY NO-BAKE CHEESECAKE

Ingredients

- 200g digestive biscuits
- 60g unsalted butter, melted
- ½ tsp vanilla extract
- 500g mascarpone
- 2 lemons, 1 zested, both juiced
- 350g condensed milk
- 500g blueberries
- mint leaves to decorate

Method

1. STEP 1 Crush the biscuits into coarse crumbs using a rolling pin. Melt the butter, then stir in the vanilla extract. It ought to resemble wet sand in texture. The remainder should be smoothed onto the base of a 28cm springform pan, saving a sizable amount for decorating. Give it 30 minutes in the refrigerator to firm up.
2. STEP 2 Mix the mascarpone, condensed milk, lemon juice, and zest in a bowl using an electric mixer or a manual whisk. Place aside.
3. STEP 3 Take the chilled biscuit base out of the fridge and top with the mascarpone mixture after adding 1/4 of the blueberries. Lift the tin and tap it on the side a few times to coat the blueberries. Add the rest of the blueberries, mint, and biscuit crumbs on top. Once stiff, chill for 2 to 3 hours.
4. We have not retested this recipe; Moje Gotowane has provided it.

4. CAPPUCCINO MOUSSE

Prep15 Min

Total30 Min

Servings6

Ingredients

- 1cup of milk
- 3/4cup of cold strong coffee
- 1package (4-serving size) vanilla instant pudding and pie filling mix
- 2tbsp sugar
- 2cups of whipping (heavy) cream
- 1/4cup of sugar

Steps

1. 1 In a large bowl, whisk the milk, coffee, dry pudding mix, and 2 tbsp of sugar for about 2 minutes, or until the mixture begins to slightly thicken.
2. 2
3. Whipping cream and 1/4 cup of sugar should be vigorously whisked together in a large, refrigeratedd bowl until firm. Whip cream into coffee mixture while stirring slowly.
4. 3 Place into every dessert dish separately. 15 minutes or until firm, place in refrigerator.

5. CARAMEL PECAN PIE

Prep Time: 15 mins

Cook Time: 55 mins

Additional Time: 15 mins

Total Time: 1 hrs 25 mins

Servings: 8

Ingredients

- 1 (9 inch) unbaked pie crust
- 36 individually wrapped caramels, unwrapped
- ¼ cup of unsalted butter
- ¼ cup of milk
- ¾ cup of white sugar
- 3 large eggs
- ½ tsp vanilla extract
- ¼ tsp salt
- 1 cup of pecan halves

Directions

1. Set the oven to 350 degrees Fahrenheit (175 degrees C.)
2. Melt butter, milk, and caramels together in a saucepan over low heat. Cook for 10 to 15 minutes, stirring often, until the caramels are melted and the liquid is smooth. Turn off the heat and leave the pot alone.
3. In a sizable bowl, mix the sugar, eggs, vanilla, and salt. Stir in the melted caramel mixture gradually before adding the pecans. Filling should be added to a raw pie crust.
4. For 45 to 50 minutes, or until the pastry is golden brown, bake in the preheated oven. Remove from the oven and allow cool for about 15 minutes on a wire rack before serving. cold or warm serving.

6. CARROT CAKE CUP OFCAKES

Prep:30 mins

Cook:22 mins

Ingredients

- 175g light muscovado sugar

- 100g wholemeal self-raising flour
- 100g self-raising flour
- 1 tsp bicarbonate of soda
- 2 tsp mixed spice
- 1 orange, zested
- 2 eggs
- 150ml sunflower oil
- 200g carrots, grated
- orange coloured sprinkles, to decorate
- For the icing
- 100g butter, softened
- 300g soft cheese
- 100g icing sugar, sifted
- 1 tsp vanilla extract

Method

1. STEP 1 Turn up the oven's temperature to 180°C/160°F fan/gas 4, then line a 12-hole muffin tray with cases. Mix the sugar, flours, baking soda, mixed spices, and zest from one orange in a sizable mixing dish. Eggs and oil should be whisked together before being added to the dry ingredients and carrot. Bake for 20 to 22 minutes, or until a skewer inserted comes out clean. Divide the mixture between the cases. Before frosting, let cool on a wire rack.
2. STEP 2 To make the icing, whip the butter until it is very soft. Add the soft cheese, icing sugar, and vanilla after that. The frosting should be swirled onto the cakes using a palette or slicelery knife, followed by the sprinkles.

7. CHOCOLATE CHERRY CAKE ROLL

Prep Time: 15 minutes

Cook Time: 15 minutes

Cooling Time: 1 hour

Servings: 8 servings

Ingredients

- For the Chocolate Cake:
- 1/2 cup of all-purpose flour
- 1/4 cup of unsweetened dark cocoa powder
- 1 tsp baking powder
- 1/2 tsp salt
- 4 eggs
- 1/2 cup of granulated sugar
- 2 Tbsp butter, melted
- 1 tsp vanilla extract
- For the Cherry Buttercream:
- 8 oz fresh red cherries, stemmed and pitted
- 3 Tbsp granulated sugar
- 1 Tbsp lemon juice
- 1 cup of unsalted butter, softened
- Pinch of salt
- 4 cups of powdered sugar
- 1 tsp almond extract

Instructions

°F oven temperature. To easily remove the cake out of the pan and roll it up after baking, line a 15 x 10-inch jelly roll pan with parchment paper, leaving an additional 1-inch of parchment sticking up on both 15-inch sides of the pan.

Flour, cocoa powder, baking powder, and salt should all be thoroughly blended in a medium bowl. Place aside.

Eggs and granulated sugar should be whisked in the bowl of a stand mixer for a minute or until thick. Whisk in the vanilla essence and melted butter just until incorporated. Add the flour mixture to the mixer and beat on low speed until just incorporated.

Fill the prepared pan equally with the batter. 11 minutes of baking time, or until cake top bounces back when touched. Lift the cake carefully from the parchment paper and onto a heat-safe, flat surface. Use your hands to slowly and carefully roll the cake starting at the short end until it is entirely rolled up (the cake will be extremely hot). After being moved to a wire rack, let the cake roll cool until room temperature.

Make the cherry buttercream filling while the cake is cooling.

Creating the Buttercream In a medium saucepan, mix the cherries, granulated sugar, and lemon juice. Cook, stirring occasionally, until the mixture boils and the juices begin to escape. For 8 to 10 minutes, or until all the cherry juices have released, keep heating and stirring while smashing the cherries with a hard spoon as they soften.

To strain the cherries, place a fine mesh strainer over a bowl and crush the cherries with the back of a spoon to extract as much juice as you can. You ought to receive roughly 1/3 cup of. Cherry juice should be put in the fridge to chill fully.

Butter and salt should be mixd on high speed for two to three minutes in the bowl of a stand mixer with a paddle attachment.

One cup of at a time, add the powdered sugar, mix on low speed until all of the powdered sugar has been added, then blend on high speed until creamy and mixed. Add the chilled cherry juice and almond extract and blend on high for two to three minutes, or until frothy.

Transfer the cake roll to a flat surface once it has cooled to room temperature. Carefully unroll the cake until it is flat once more (the ends may have curled slightly, but that's good!). Spread a layer of cherry buttercream over the cake that is about 1/2" thick, leaving a border of about 1/2 inch on both sides. Reroll the cake carefully, gradually removing the parchment paper as you go until you can discard it entirely. Refrigerate for at least an hour after tightly wrapping the chocolate roll in plastic wrap.

The chocolate roll should be taken out, unwrapped, and placed in your serving dish. Sprinkle with a little icing sugar, then if desired*, top with more cherry buttercream and fresh cherries. Serve the slices!

Simply rewrap the chocolate roll in plastic wrap and put it in the refrigerator for up to three days if you have leftovers.

Notes

1. *Delay placing anything on top of the roll, rewrap it in plastic wrap, and refrigerated if you won't be serving it straight away. When you're ready to serve, decorate and slice!

Nutrition

2. Serving size is 1 slice with 616 calories, 90 grams of carbohydrates, 5 grams of protein, 28 grams of fat, 17 grams of saturated fat, 150 mg of sodium, 149 mg of potassium, 2 grams of fiber, 80 grams of sugar, 60 mg of calcium, and 1 mg of iron per slice.

8. CHOCOLATE-ORANGE BREAD PUDDING

Total: 1 hr 10 min

Active: 20 min

Ingredients

- Deselect All
- Pudding:
- Nonstick cooking spray, for the baking dish
- 4 large eggs
- 1 cup of whole milk
- 1/2 cup of heavy cream
- 3 tbsp granulated sugar
- 1 tsp pure vanilla extract
- 1/4 tsp kosher salt
- 6 cups of bread cubes (1-inch cubes), such as sourdough
- 1/2 cup of dark chocolate chips
- Sauce:
- 1 cup of orange juice, fresh or store-bought
- 1/4 cup of granulated sugar
- 1/4 cup of packed light brown sugar
- 1 tbsp cornstarch
- 1 navel orange, zested

Directions

3. For the mash: Set the oven to 350 degrees Fahrenheit. A 2-quart baking dish should receive a light coating of nonstick cooking spray.

4. In a sizable bowl, stir the eggs, milk, cream, sugar, vanilla, and salt. Bread and chocolate chips should be added. Toss the bread and chocolate until evenly distributed and covered on all sides. Fill the baking dish with the liquid. Bake for 45 to 50 minutes, or until puffed and golden brown.

5. To make the sauce: Place a small saucepot over medium-high heat in the interim. 1 tbsp of the orange juice should be set aside. Whisk the remaining orange juice and sugars together in the saucepot. Simmer for about 10 minutes, stirring occasionally, until the sugars are dissolved.

6. In a separate dish, stir together the cornstarch and orange juice that was set aside. Pour into the sauce and stir to incorporate. Cook for about 5 minutes, or until the sauce thickens to a syrup. Add the orange zest and stir. As it cools, the sauce will get even thicker. After serving the pudding, drizzle the heated sauce over it.

9. CHOCOLATE TORTE

Ingredients

- METRIC
- IMPERIAL
- CHOCOLATE TORTE
- 225g of 70% dark chocolate, broken into pieces
- 160g of ground almonds
- 140g of white breadcrumbs, dried
- 225g of unsalted butter
- 340g of caster sugar
- 6 medium free-range eggs
- 1 drop of vanilla essence
- BISCUIT BASE
- 175g of digestive biscuits

- 1 tbsp of cocoa powder
- 85g of butter, melted
- CHOCOLATE GANACHE
- 110g of 70% dark chocolate, broken into pieces
- 225ml of double cream
- 125g of icing sugar

Method

1. 1 Greaseproof paper should be used to line the cake pan as the oven is preheated to 160°C/gas mark 3.
2. 2 Blend the biscuits and cocoa powder to a fine crumb to create the biscuit base. The butter should be added and then thoroughly mixed. Spread the ingredients evenly across the cake pan after spooning it in.
3. 175 grams of digestive cookies
4. Cocoa powder, 1 tbsp
5. 85 grams of melted butter
6. 3
7. To prepare the torte, melt the chocolate in a bain-marie and then stir in the breadcrumbs and ground almonds. In a another bowl, cream the butter and sugar until frothy. Add the eggs one at a time, then the vanilla. Then, add the chocolate mixture to the butter and eggs, and stir everything together until well-mixd. Fill the cake pan with the mixture, and bake for 55 minutes, or until set and well cooked. Observe cooling
8. 225g of broken-down 70% dark chocolate
9. 140 grams of dry white breadcrumbs
10. 160g of almond meal
11. Sugar, caster, 340 grams
12. Unsalted butter, 225g
13. Vanilla essence, 1 drop
14. 6 medium eggs, free-range
15. 4

16. Put the chocolate in a big basin to make the chocolate ganache. In a saucepan, bring the cream and icing sugar to a boil. Pour the hot mixture over the chocolate, whisking to mix the ingredients and melt the chocolate. Leave alone to cool

17. Double cream in 225ml

18. 110g of broken-down 70% dark chocolate

19. 125 grams of sugar

20. 5 Using a heated palette knife to ensure even distribution, spread the ganache over the chilled chocolate torte. Slice the torte after the ganache has hardened, then serve it with extra-thick double cream and raspberries.

21. a single punnet of raspberries

10. CINNAMON BREAD PUDDING

Prep Time 25 mins

Cook Time 40 mins

Ingredients

- 10-12 slices Brioche bread, cubed You can use regular white bread too
- 70 gms (1/2 cup of) Raisins
- 35 gms (1/3 cups of) Pecan, roughly chop up
- 3 Eggs
- 350 ml (1 1/2 cups of) Coconut milk You can use any milk you prefer
- 170 gms (3/4 cup of) Raw sugar You can use white sugar
- 1 tsp Vanilla extract
- tsp Cinnamon powder
- 1 tbsp Butter, melted
- 2 tsp Cinnamon sugar, for topping Non-compulsory
- Ice cream and caramel sauce for serving Non-compulsory

Instructions

1. In a sizable bowl, mix the bread, raisins, and pecans.
2. In a small bowl, mix the eggs, coconut milk, sugar, vanilla essence, and cinnamon powder.
3. the bread mixture with the liquid.
4. To help the bread properly absorb the custard mixture, slightly press it down.
5. For the custard to soak up most of the liquid, let the mixture stand for 10 to 15 minutes.
6. Set the oven to 180°C.
7. In a pan with an 8- or 9-inch diameter, pour the bread mixture. I employed two tiny baking dishes.
8. Spread the melted butter over top and top with some cinnamon sugar.
9. Bake the pudding for 35 to 40 minutes, or until the custard is set and the top is golden brown.
10. Serve warm with ice cream and caramel sauce on the side. Enjoy!

11. COCONUT CREAM PIE RECIPE

Ingredients

- 1 pie crust recipe
- FOR THE TOASTED COCONUT TOPPING
- 1/2 cup of flaked sweetened coconut
- FOR THE COCONUT CUSTARD
- 1 1/2 cups of canned coconut milk
- 1 1/2 cups of half-and-half
- 5 egg yolks
- 3/4 cup of sugar
- 4 tbsp cornstarch

- 1 tbsp butter
- 1/4 tsp salt
- 1 1/2 cups of flaked sweetened coconut
- 1 1/2 tsp vanilla
- Whipped Cream

Instructions

1. Pie crust should be made in accordance with the recipe's blind-baking directions.
2. RELATING TO THE TOASTED COCONUT TOPPING
3. On a baking sheet with a rim, spread the coconut evenly. Place coconut in a 350° F oven for 8 to 10 minutes, or until it just starts to turn golden.
4. Set apart for cooling.
5. PURPOSES OF THE COCONUT CUSTARD
6. Fill a liquid measuring cup of with half-and-half and coconut milk. Add the egg yolks and mix the milks in the mixer. Place aside.
7. Over medium-low heat, mix sugar and cornstarch in a heavy-bottomed saucepan. Re-whisk the egg and milk mixture, and then add the sugar and cornstarch gradually while still whisking.
8. To boil the custard mixture. Use a wooden spoon or a rubber spatula now, and stir continuously. 1 minute of boiling.
9. Add butter, coconut, vanilla, and salt after taking the pan off the heat.
10. In the pie crust, spread custard. Refrigerate until solid, about 30-45 minutes, then lightly cover with plastic wrap.
11. Whipping cream should be topped with coconut custard. Keep chilled until you're ready to serve.
12. Add toasted coconut over top when ready to serve.

12. COCONUT MILKSHAKE

PREP TIME 5 mins

COOK TIME 0 mins

TOTAL TIME 5 mins

INGREDIENTS

- 2 cups of coconut cream from the can
- 1 cup of vanilla ice cream or vegan vanilla ice cream
- 1 cup of unsweetened coconut milk or any milk
- 4 ice cubes non-compulsory
- 2 tsp sugar non-compulsory

INSTRUCTIONS

1. Blend all the ingredients—except the sugar—in a high-speed blender until they are thoroughly mixd.

2. If necessary, increase the sweetness by adding sugar. If you add sugar, make sure to blend the milkshake for 1-2 minutes to fully incorporate it.

3. If additional coconut milk is required, adjust the consistency by doing so.

4. Serve right away. Put a dollop of ice cream on top to make the dish even more delectable!

13. CREAM CHEESE POUND CAKE

Prep Time: 15 minutes

Cook Time: 1 hour, 20 minutes

Total Time: 4 hours

Ingredients

- 1 and 1/2 cups of (3 sticks; 345g) unsalted butter, softened to room temperature
- 8 ounce (226g) block full-fat cream cheese, softened to room temperature
- 2 and 1/2 cups of (500g) granulated sugar
- 1/3 cup of (80g) sour cream, at room temperature
- 2 tsp pure vanilla extract
- 6 large eggs, at room temperature
- 3 cups of (354g) cake flour (spoon & leveled)
- 1/2 tsp baking powder
- 1/8 tsp salt
- non-compulsory for serving: homemade whipped cream & fresh berries

Instructions

1. oven to 325°F (163°C) before using. Not 350°F. Grease a 10 to 12-cup of Bundt pan well with butter or nonstick spray.

2. Beat the butter on high speed for two minutes, either with a hand-held or stand mixer equipped with a paddle or whisk attachment. Use a rubber spatula to scrape the bowl's bottom and sides clean. Add the cream cheese and beat on high speed for about a minute, or until everything is thoroughly blended and smooth. After adding the sugar and beating on high speed for approximately a minute to mix, add the sour cream and vanilla and continue beating until smooth. Use a rubber spatula to scrape the bowl's bottom and sides clean.

3. Beat the eggs in one at a time on low speed, letting every thoroughly incorporate before adding the next. After adding the eggs, take care not to overmix. Stop the mixer once the sixth egg has been mixed, then add the cake flour, baking soda, and salt. Just until mixd, beat at medium speed. Avoid overmixing. Give the batter one last stir with a rubber spatula or firm whisk to ensure there are no lumps at the bottom of the basin. The batter will be very creamy and slightly thick.

4. Pour or spoon the batter into the pan as directed. To release any air bubbles, lightly tap the pan against the counter a few times. 75 to 95 minutes of baking. To prevent the top from over-browning, loosely tent the baking cake with aluminum foil halfway through the baking period. A low and slow baking time is essential for pound cake. Check for doneness with a toothpick. The pound cake is finished when the toothpick is entirely clean. Don't be concerned if it takes longer in your oven because this is a big, thick cake. Bake it for longer if necessary.

5. Take the cake out of the oven and let it cool in the pan for two hours. Then, flip the pound cake that has only partially cooled onto a wire rack or serving plate. Allow to totally cool.

6. Slice and serve with extras like fresh berries and homemade whipped cream.

7. Cake leftovers should be properly covered and kept for up to 2 days at room temperature or up to 5 days in the refrigerator.

14. DARK CHOCOLATE COFFEE CUP OFCAKES

PREP TIME30 mins

COOK TIME30 mins

TOTAL TIME1 hr

Ingredients

- ounces semi-sweet chocolate , fine-quality dark chocolate, such as Lindt chocolate bar (70% cacao)
- 1 ½ cups of brewed coffee , hot
- 3 cups of sugar
- 2 ½ cups of all-purpose flour
- 1 ½ cups of unsweetened cocoa powder
- 2 tsp baking soda
- 1 tsp baking powder
- 1 tsp salt
- 3 large eggs
- ¾ cup of vegetable oil
- 1 ½ cups of buttermilk , well-shaken
- 1 tsp vanilla extract

Instructions

1. Set the oven to 350 degrees.

2. Slice the chocolate bar into tiny pieces. In this recipe, I used a 70% cocoa Lindt chocolate bar, and it turned out great.

3. Stir the hot coffee and lightly chop up chocolate together in a small bowl, then set the mixture aside until the chocolate has completely melted.

4. Add sugar, flour, cocoa powder, baking soda, and baking powder to a large bowl and thoroughly mix.

5. Using a hand-held mixer, beat 3 eggs in a separate large bowl for about 3 minutes, or until they are frothy, thickened, and just beginning to foam.

6. Add the melted chocolate coffee mixture, buttermilk, oil, and vanilla; whisk everything together until well mixd.

7. Mixture of flour, cocoa powder, and sugar should be added to the wet components. Mix with a mixer just until mixd. Avoid overmixing.

8. Put liners in muffin tins or cup ofcake pans.

9. Fill muffin tins or cup ofcake pans with batter so that every one is about two-thirds full. Due to the dough's tendency to rise while baking, refrain from filling them all the way to the top.

10. Cup ofcakes should be baked for 20 to 30 minutes, or until a toothpick inserted in the center of one comes out clean.

15. GERMAN CHOCOLATE CAKE BARS

prep time: 10 MINS

cook time: 25 MINS

total time: 35 MINS

servings: 16 BARS

INGREDIENTS

- CRUST:
- 1 (18.25 ounce) box devil's good cake mix
- 1/2 cup of (1 stick) unsalted butter, melted
- 1 large egg
- FILLING:
- 1 (14 oz) can sweetened condensed milk

- 1 tsp vanilla extract
- 1 large egg
- 1 cup of chop up pecans
- 1 cup of shredded sweetened coconut
- 1/2 cup of milk chocolate chips

INSTRUCTIONS

1. Set the oven's temperature to 350. A 9x13 inch baking pan should be greased or sprayed with cooking spray.
2. Cake mix, butter, and egg should be mixd in a medium bowl before being pressed into the bottom of the prepared pan. After 7 minutes of baking, turn off the oven. In the following stage, the crust will continue to bake.
3. Mix the sweetened condensed milk, vanilla, egg, pecans, and coconut while the crust bakes. Sprinkle the chocolate chips equally over the pour and the heated crust. Bake the top for 24 to 30 minutes, or until it turns a pale golden brown. Avoid overbaking! After removing from the oven, let the squares cool fully before sliceting.

16. GINGERBREAD SOUFFLÉS

Total: 1 hr 30 mins

Ingredients

- Ingredient Checklist
- 1 cup of milk
- ½ cup of sugar
- ¼ cup of all-purpose flour
- ¼ tsp salt
- ⅓ cup of molasses

- 2 tbsp butter, softened
- 2 tsp pumpkin pie spice
- 1 tsp ground ginger
- 2 tsp vanilla extract
- 6 large eggs, separated
- ⅛ tsp cream of tartar
- Sweetened whipped cream, crushed gingersnaps

Directions

1. the oven to 350 degrees. In a medium saucepan, mix the first 4 ingredients and whisk until smooth. Over medium heat, while whisking continuously, bring to a boil. Whisk in molasses and the following 4 ingredients after transferring mixture to a sizable bowl. 15 minutes to cool. Add egg yolks and stir.

2. 10 (7-oz.) ramekins with butter; sprinkle with sugar to coat, shaking off extra.

3. With an electric mixer set to high speed, beat the egg whites and cream of tartar until firm peaks form. After thoroughly blending, fold one-third of the egg white mixture into the milk mixture. With the remaining egg white mixture, repeat twice. Fill every ramekin with batter, leaving a 3/4-inch space at the top.

4. Bake for 25 minutes at 350 degrees, or until puffy and set. Serve right away with whipped cream and gingersnaps that have been crushed.

5. Remarkably, you could also bake this in a 2-1/2-quart soufflé dish. 55 to 60 minutes of baking time, or until fluffy and set.

17. LEMON MERINGUE ICE CREAM

Prep:10 mins - 20 mins

Ingredients

- 500g carton fresh custard
- 142ml carton single cream
- 142ml carton double cream
- zest and juice of 3 juicy lemons, unwaxed if possible
- 6 good quality meringues, crushed (we used Sainsbury's Meringue Nests)
- 8 good quality ice cream cones

Method

1. STEP 1 Mix the custard and the single cream in a big bowl.
2. STEP 2 Stir the lemon zest and juice into the double cream after whipping it to soft peaks. To the custard mixture, fold this in.
3. Step three is to pour the mixture into an ice cream maker and churn it as directed by the manufacturer. Meringue should be folded in gently before being spooned into a freezer container and refrigerated. At least 30 minutes before serving, take the refrigerated food out of the freezer. Scoop the ice cream into cones and devour right away to serve.

18. MINI BREAD PUDDINGS

Serves: 6

Prep Time: 8 min

Cook Time: 20 min

Ingredients

- 4eggs

- ½ cup of (125 mL)milk (1%)
- ½ cup of (125 mL)granulated sugar
- 1 1/2 tsp (7.5 mL)vanilla extract
- 2 1/2 cups of (625 mL)cinnamon raisin bread cubes (about 1/2-inch/1.5 cm)
- ⅔ cup of (170 mL)chop up dried apple and/or cranberries

Instructions

1. Oven should be heated to 350°F (180°C).
2. In a big bowl, whisk the eggs, milk, sugar, and vanilla. Bread cubes and dried fruit are mixd.
3. Using paper baking cups of or cooking spray, line a 6-muffin pan. Mixture should be filled to the brim of the glasses.
4. Bake for 20 minutes or until knife inserted in center comes out clean in a 350°F (180°C) oven.

19. MINI KEY LIME PIES

Prep Time: 30 minutes

Cook Time: 20 minutes

Total Time: 3 hours, 45 minutes

Ingredients

- 1 and 1/2 cups of (180g) graham cracker crumbs (about 12 full sheet graham crackers)
- 6 Tbsp (85g) unsalted butter, melted
- 1/4 cup of (50g) granulated sugar
- Filling
- 4 ounces (112g) full-fat cream cheese, softened to room temperature
- 4 large egg yolks

- one 14-ounce can (396g) full-fat sweetened condensed milk
- 1/2 cup of (120ml) key lime juice*
- non-compulsory: lime slices and whipped cream for garnish

Instructions

1. Set the oven's temperature to 350°F (177°C). Separately, line a second 12-count muffin tray with only four liners (since this recipe makes only around 16). Discard the pans.
2. creating the crust Here are all of my suggestions for making the ideal graham cracker crust before you get started. You can ground up whole graham crackers in a food processor or blender if you're starting out with them. Or use a rolling pin to smash them in a bag with a zippered cover. With a rubber spatula, mix the graham cracker crumbs, melted butter, and granulated sugar in a medium bowl. The mixture will be sand-like, thick, and grainy. Every liner should be filled with a heaping Tbsp of the mixture, and the crust should be compact and tight. There could be some crust left behind. If so, you can add a bit additional pressure to every liner. Bake the crusts for 5 minutes beforehand. From the oven, remove.
3. Creating the filling Cream cheese should be beaten on high speed for about a minute in a large basin using a hand-held or stand mixer with a whisk attachment. Add the egg yolks and beat on medium-high speed, scraping down the sides as necessary. Beat the sweetened condensed milk and lime juice together until well-mixd on high speed.
4. Fill every crust evenly with the filling. Bake for 15 to 16 minutes, or until the pies' centers jiggle just a little bit (I do this by shaking the muffin tray around in the oven while wearing an oven mitt!). The pies should be allowed to cool in the pan on a wire rack at room temperature. Place the pan in the refrigerator for at least two hours and up to a day once it has totally cooled.
5. When the key lime pies are chilled, serve them cold with whipped cream and a lime slice if you like. Pie leftovers can be kept for up to a week in the refrigerator (covered). if they persist for so long!

20. BUTTER CAKE

Prep Time 20 minutes

Cook Time 1 hour

Total Time 1 hour 20 minutes

Ingredients

- For the Cake:
- 3 cups of all-purpose flour (360g)
- 1 tsp salt
- ¾ tsp baking powder
- ½ tsp baking soda
- 1 cup of unsalted butter softened (227g)
- 2 cups of granulated sugar (400g)
- 4 large eggs
- 1 cup of whole milk (240ml)
- For the Glaze:
- 5 tbsp unsalted butter (70g)
- ¾ cup of granulated sugar (150g)
- ¼ cup of water (60ml)
- 1½ tsp vanilla extract

Instructions

1. Set the oven to 325°F and prepare the cake. A 10- to 12-cup of Bundt pan should be butter and floured.
2. Mix the flour, salt, baking soda, and baking powder in a big bowl.
3. Beat the butter and sugar at medium speed in a sizable mixing bowl or with a stand mixer equipped with a paddle attachment for three to four minutes, pausing occasionally to scrape the bowl's sides. Add the eggs one at a time, beating well after every addition while running the mixer on low.
4. With the mixer running on low, gradually add the flour mixture to the butter mixture in pairs, beginning and finishing with the flour mixture, and beat every addition just until incorporated. In the preheated pan, pour the batter.
5. A wooden pick inserted close to the center should come out clean after baking for an hour.

6. For the Glaze, mix the butter, sugar, and water in a small saucepan as soon as the cake comes out of the oven. Over medium heat, bring to a simmer while stirring continuously. Cook for about 2 minutes, stirring regularly, until opaque and just beginning to thicken. Add the vanilla after taking the pot off the heat.

7. Pour on top of the pan-bound cake. Allow 15 minutes for cooling. Before serving, flip the cake over onto a wire rack to finish cooling. The cake can be kept at room temperature, covered, for up to 5 days.

21. NO-BAKE CHOCOLATE SWIRL CHEESECAKE

Total Time: 54 minute

INGREDIENTS

- For the Crust
- 1 1/2 cups of graham cracker crumbs
- 5 tbsp unsalted butter, melted
- 1/4 cup of granulated sugar
- 1 tsp kosher salt
- For the Filling
- 2 8z packages full-fat cream cheese, room temp
- 1 14oz can (1 1/4 cups of) sweetened condensed milk
- 1 tsp vanilla extract
- 5 oz dark chocolate (I used 70%), roughly chop up

INSTRUCTIONS

1. As for the Crust
2. The graham cracker crumbs, sugar, salt, and melted butter should all be mixd in a medium basin. Stir mixture just until it resembles wet sand. Spread the crumb mixture 1 1/2 to 2 inches up the side of a

9-inch springform pan. Spend 15 minutes freezing the crust. As an alternative, you can bake the crust for 10 minutes at 350F before letting it cool.

3. In Order to Fill

4. In a heatproof bowl placed over a pot of simmering water, melt the chocolate (double-broiler). As the chocolate melts and becomes shiny and smooth, stir it occasionally. Remove from heat slowly, being careful not to spill any water into the bowl.

5. To create the filling, beat the softened cream cheese until it is smooth in the bowl of a stand mixer fitted with the paddle attachment at medium speed. Beat on low speed while adding the condensed milk and vanilla.

6. Spread the melted chocolate on top of the filling after pouring it over the cold crust. Swirl the filling 2-3 times with a skewer or knife using an 8-figure pattern.

7. Before serving, wrap the dish in plastic wrap and place it in the refrigerator for 2-4 hours.

22. NO BAKE LEMON TART

Prep Time20 mins

Servings6

Ingredients

- For the base
- 8 oz Digestive biscuits or Graham Crackers – we like a thick base as it holds better, but you can use half the amount if you like a thinner base
- ½ cup of Unsalted butter
- 2 tbsp Caster sugar
- For the filling
- 12 oz Condensed milk
- 1¼ cups of Heavy cream (double)
- 2 Large lemons zest and juice
- Topping

- The zest or slices of a lemon this is non-compulsory

Instructions

the foundation

The biscuits should be placed in a zippered bag (we use sandwich bags) before being gently crushed with a rolling pin.

oz Healthy biscuits

Melt the butter in a pan, then stir in the sugar and gradually add the biscuit crumbs. If you are using small cases, press the crumb mixture firmly into your dish or dishes. Non-compulsory: If you want the bases to be more stable, bake them at 160°C/320°F for 8 minutes, then remove them from the oven and let them cool.

tbsp. Caster sugar and 1/2 cup of unsalted butter

In order to fill

Condensed milk, heavy cream, and freshly grated lemon zest should all be mixd in a mixing dish. Incorporate both lemons' juice gradually, a bit at a time, while whisking constantly until it thickens.

Condensed milk, 1 1/4 cups of, 12 oz. Double heavy cream, two large lemons

Pour the mixture into the dish(es) after the base(s) have cooled, and then place the dish(es) in the refrigerator to set for at least three hours, ideally overnight. Add lemon zest or slices as a garnish.

slices or zest of a lemon

Serve and savor the super-simple, super-lemony food!

Nutrition

1. 694kcal, 69g of carbohydrates, 9g of protein, 44g of fat, 26g of saturated fat, 3g of polyunsaturated fat, 13g of monounsaturated fat, 1g of trans fat, 133mg of cholesterol, 275mg of sodium, 359mg of potassium, 48g of sugar, 222mg of calcium, and 2mg of iron make up this serving.

23. PEVERY CUSTARD TART

Ingredients

- CRUST
- 1/2 cup of Land O Lakes® Butter, softened
- 1/3 cup of sugar
- 1 1/4 cups of all-purpose flour
- 1/2 tsp almond extract
- FILLING
- 3 large (3 cups of) peaches, peel off, split
- 1/2 cup of sugar
- 1/4 cup of Land O Lakes® Heavy Whipping Cream
- 1 tbsp all-purpose flour
- 1 large Land O Lakes® Egg
- 2 tbsp split almonds

How to make

2. STEP 1 Turn on the oven to 400°F.
3. STEP 2 In a bowl, mix butter and 1/3 cup of sugar. Beat until creamy at medium speed while often scraping the bowl. Mix well after adding 1 1/4 cups of flour and almond extract while beating at low speed.
4. STEP 3 Press dough into a 9-inch tart pan with a removable bottom and up the sides. Use a fork to prick the crust's sides and bottom. Bake for 15 to 18 minutes, or until a pale golden brown color. Place peach slices over the hot, partially baked crust after taking it out of the oven.
5. STEP 4 Lower the oven's heat setting to 350°F.
6. STEP 5 In a bowl, whisk together the other filling ingredients, excluding the almonds. Overlay the peach slices with the filling mixture and top with slice almonds. Bake for 32 to 40 minutes, or until the filling is firmed up and the crust is golden. Complete cooling. Keep cool when storing.

24. OLD-FASHIONED FRESH PEVERY ICE CREAM

PREP TIME 30 mins

COOK TIME 8 mins

ADDITIONAL TIME 4 hrs

TOTAL TIME 4 hrs 38 mins

INGREDIENTS

- 3 medium peaches peel off and split (about 2 cups of)
- 1 ¼ cup of sugar separated
- ½ tsp lemon juice
- ¼ tsp salt
- 5 large egg yolks
- 1 ½ cup of heavy cream
- 1 ½ cups of whole milk
- 1 tsp vanilla

INSTRUCTIONS

1. Peveryes should be peel off and slice into slices before being mixd with 1/2 cup of sugar and lemon juice in a large basin. For 30 to 60 minutes, let the peaches sit at room temperature until they are soft and have released their juices to produce a syrupy liquid.

2. Once the peaches have exuded their juices, mash them with a fork or potato masher until only tiny bits of peach are left. Large, individual peach slices will freeze very hard if you put them in your ice cream. Reserving the juice as well as the mashed peaches, strain the juice into a different bowl, and then chill it until you're ready to use it.

3. In the meantime, mix the cream, milk, remaining 1/2 cup of sugar, and salt in a medium pot. Heat to a high but not bubbling temperature over a medium-low heat.

4. The egg yolks and remaining 1/4 cup of sugar should be whisked together in a large bowl for two minutes or until light in color.

5. To temper the eggs before adding them to the custard foundation, whisk 12 cup of the hot cream mixture into the egg yolk and sugar mixture. Add a further 1/2 cup of hot cream gradually while continuously whisking.

6. When the mixture is between 170 and 175 degrees and just thick enough to coat the back of the spoon, add the tempered egg yolks to the saucepan along with the remaining custard foundation. Stir gently for 2-4 minutes. Add the vanilla after taking the pan off the heat.

7. Pour the custard base through a fine mesh strainer into a clean basin, stir in the mashed peach liquor, and chill the mixture in the fridge for 4 hours or until completely cooled.

8. Following the manufacturer's instructions, pour the peach ice cream base into the ice cream machine and churn it for 25 to 30 minutes, or until it resembles soft-serve ice cream. Towards the end of the churning process, stir in the reserved crushed peaches. After that, transfer the ice cream to an airtight container and freeze for at least 4-6 hours to ripen.

25. PEANUT BUTTER PIE

Prep Time: 20 mins

Additional Time: 2 hrs

Total Time: 2 hrs 20 mins

Servings: 8

Ingredients

- 1 (8 ounce) package cream cheese, softened
- ½ cup of creamy peanut butter
- ½ cup of confectioners' sugar
- 1 (16 ounce) container refrigerated whipped topping, thawed, separated
- 1 (9 inch) prepared graham cracker crust
- 15 miniature chocolate-covered peanut butter cups of (such as Reese's®), unwrapped

Directions

1. Confectioners' sugar, cream cheese, and peanut butter should all be thoroughly mixd. After incorporating half of the whipped topping, spoon the finished product into the graham cracker crust.

2. Sprinkle peanut butter cups of on top of the leftover whipped topping and peanut butter mixture. Before serving, chill for at least two hours or overnight.

26. POMEGRANATE PANNA COTTA

prep time2 HOURS

cook time5 MINUTES

total time2 HOURS 5 MINUTES

INGREDIENTS

- 1/2 cup of (118 ml) heavy cream
- Juice and zest of 1 orange
- 1 tsp granulated sugar
- 1/2 tsp good vanilla extract
- 1 1/2 cups of (354 ml) whole milk
- 1 tbsp powdered gelatin
- 1 1/2 cups of (354 ml) pomegranate juice
- 1 tbsp powdered gelatin
- 2 tsp granulated sugar
- Seeds of 1 pomegranate, for garnish

INSTRUCTIONS

1. Over medium heat, mix the cream, orange juice, and rind in a saucepan. Simmer after adding the sugar. After adding the vanilla, stir.

2. Pour the milk into a small bowl, then add the gelatin. Give it about five minutes to soften. The gelatin and milk should be well dissolved in the cream.

3. Pour the mixture into the glasses and tilt them within a muffin pan or an empty egg carton. Set in the refrigerator for at least two hours, preferably overnight.

4. In the meantime, add 1 tbsp of gelatin to the pomegranate juice and let it sit in a measuring cup of for 5 minutes to dissolve. Add to a skillet with sugar and heat until simmering. Allow it slightly cool before pouring back into the measuring cup of and dousing the prepared panna cotta. Keep chilled until set.

5. Add pomegranate seeds as a garnish.

27. SUGARED PECAN PUMPKIN ICE CREAM

Ingredients

- Ice Cream
- 2 large eggs
- 3/4 cup of sugar
- 2 cups of heavy cream or whipping cream
- 1 cup of milk
- 1 cup of unsweetened canned pumpkin
- 1 tsp freshly grated nutmeg
- 1 tsp ground cinnamon
- 1 cup of coarsely broken sugared pecan halves
- Sugared Pecans
- 2 pounds shelled pecan halves
- 2 egg whites
- 2 tsp cold water
- 1 cup of sugar
- 2 tsp cinnamon

- 1/2 tsp salt
- 1/2 tsp freshly grated nutmeg

Instructions

1. Icy treat
2. In a saucepan, mix the milk and cream; cook over low heat.
3. Separately, beat the eggs in a medium mixing bowl until they are light and fluffy.
4. Once the sugar has been well incorporated into the egg mixture, continue to whisk for an additional 1 to 2 minutes.
5. Remove from heat when the cream/milk combination reaches 140°.
6. The hot cream/milk combination should be added to the egg/sugar mixture in small amounts and whisked in quickly until incorporated. (By doing so, the eggs are "tempered" and won't scramble when added.)
7. Include the rest of the cream/milk combination once it has been fully mixed.
8. Custard should be returned to the sauce pan and heated over low heat until it reaches 175 degrees. (This eliminates any dangerous microorganisms.)
9. Mixture must be thoroughly chilled to a minimum of 40°. (You should get it really cold so that it will freeze in the ice cream maker.)
10. Transfer one cup of the egg/cream mixture into a mixing basin.
11. Stir in the pumpkin, nutmeg, and cinnamon after adding them.
12. Blend thoroughly after adding pumpkin mixture to remaining cream base.
13. Transfer to an ice cream machine and proceed as directed by the manufacturer.
14. Add sugared pecans once the mixture is almost refrigerated.
15. Eat soft or freeze for 4-6 hours to make hard.
16. Sweetened Pecans
17. Pecans should be put in a sizable mixing dish.
18. Separately, whisk together egg whites and cold water.
19. Pour over the pecans and thoroughly mix.
20. Add remaining ingredients, including salt, nutmeg, sugar, and cinnamon.

21. A sizable baking or roasting pan should be used.
22. For 1.5 hours, bake uncovered at 225 degrees.
23. Every 30 minutes, stir.
24. Store in an airtight jar after cooling.

28. RASPBERRY-ALMOND CLAFOUTI

Ready In: 1hr 10mins

INGREDIENTS

- 1/2pint ripe raspberries
- 2/3cup of creme fraiche or 2/3 cup of sour cream
- 1/3cup of whole milk
- 1/2cup of unsalted butter, melted and cooled (separated)
- 3large eggs
- 1/2tsp pure vanilla bean paste or 1/2 tsp vanilla extract
- 3/4cup of cake flour
- 1/2cup of sugar (separated)
- salt, a pinch
- 1/4cup of split unblanched almonds

DIRECTIONS

1. 400° oven preheat.
2. Butter a 9-inch glass pie plate with a deep dish.
3. In the pie plate, add raspberries; reserve.

4. Blend or process the cream fraiche, milk, eggs, vanilla, 6 tbsp of butter, and other ingredients until thoroughly mixd.

5. In a bowl, mix the flour, salt, and 1/3 cup of sugar.

6. Just until mixd, whisk in the creme fraiche mixture.

7. Over the raspberries, pour the batter.

8. Add the final 2 tbsp of butter, followed by the remaining 2 tbsp of sugar and the almonds.

9. 40 minutes, or until golden brown, in the oven.

10. Serve warm after letting stand for 10 to 15 minutes on a wire rack.

29. CHOCOLATE RASPBERRY SOUFFLES

Ingredients:

- ¼ cup of butter, unsalted
- 2 oz. semi-sweet chocolate chips
- 1 egg + 1 egg yolk
- 2 tbsp brown sugar
- 2 tsp all-purpose flour
- 1 cup of fresh raspberries, washed and dried
- Confectioners sugar

Instructions:

1. To prepare the batter, melt the butter and chocolate together in a small pot. At room temperature, allow the mixture to cool. While waiting, use a stand mixer to beat the egg, egg yolk, and brown sugar on medium speed for 3–4 minutes, or until light. Beat in the chocolate mixture. The flour is folded in.

2. Prepare a standard-sized cup ofcake pan with liners or use a silicone cup ofcake pan to bake souffles. Among the six cup ofcake liners, distribute the raspberries. Add a sixth of the chocolate batter on top of the raspberries. The sweets should bake for 12 to 15 minutes at 450 degrees. To complete cooling, immediately invert onto a cooling rack.

3. Add whipped cream and a raspberry on top, then garnish with powdered sugar.

30. LEMON RASPBERRY CHEESECAKE BARS

prep time:30 MINS

cook time:45 MINS

cooling time:3 HRS

total time:4 HRS 15 MINS

INGREDIENTS

- 9 full-sheet (135 grams) graham crackers (or 1 and ¼ cups of graham cracker crumbs)
- 1/4 cup of (60 grams) butter , melted
- 2 tbsp (25 grams) granulated sugar
- FOR THE CHEESECAKE FILLING:
- 16 ounces brick-style cream cheese , softened to room temperature
- 1/2 cup of (100 grams) granulated sugar
- 1 tsp vanilla extract
- 1/4 cup of (60ml) lemon juice
- Zest of 1 lemon (1 tbsp)
- 2 large eggs , room temperature
- FOR THE RASPBERRY SWIRL:

- 1/2 cup of (65 grams) raspberries
- 1 tbsp (13 grams) granulated sugar

INSTRUCTIONS

1. HOW TO MAKE A CRUST
2. Set the oven to 325 F. Aluminum foil or parchment paper should be used to line an 8-inch square baking pan. Make sure to leave enough overhang for easy removal. Place aside.
3. You should have fine crumbs after processing the Graham crackers in a food processor. Scoop the crumbs into a mixing basin, then add the sugar and melted butter and whisk everything together thoroughly.
4. Scoop the mixture into the pan and press it down firmly to spread it out evenly.
5. Bake for ten minutes at 325 F. Take the food out of the oven, then leave it to cool. Maintain a 325°F oven temperature.
6. A CHEESECAKE FILLING IS MADE BY:
7. Beat the cream cheese until smooth in a sizable mixing basin with a handheld mixer or in a stand mixer fitted with the paddle attachment.
8. When everything is thoroughly blended, add the sugar, vanilla, lemon juice, and lemon zest. Take breaks as necessary to scrape down the bowl's edges.
9. On low speed, blend in every egg until barely incorporated.
10. Over the graham cracker shell, pour the cheesecake filling.
11. SO AS TO ENSURE RASPBERRY SWIRL
12. Blend or mix the raspberries and sugar in a food processor until smooth. To remove any seeds, pour the raspberry puree into a basin using a fine mesh strainer.
13. Use a knife to gently swirl the raspberry mixture after spooning it in various locations on top of the filling.
14. About 35 minutes or until the cheesecake's top is set, bake at 325°F.
15. Refrigerate for at least three hours or overnight after letting the food cool completely.
16. Square it up and enjoy!

31. PEVERY RASPBERRY COBBLER

Prep Time: 15 mins

Cook Time: 45 mins

Total Time: 1 hrs

Servings: 12

Ingredients

- 4 cups of split fresh peaches
- ½ cup of fresh raspberries
- ¼ cup of sugar
- 1 tsp ground cinnamon
- 1 tbsp fresh lemon juice
- ½ cup of butter
- 1 ¼ cups of all-purpose flour
- 2 tbsp baking powder
- ½ tsp salt
- 1 cup of sugar
- 1 cup of milk

Directions

1. Peveryes, raspberries, 1/4 cup of sugar, cinnamon, and lemon juice should all be mixd in a bowl. Sit while carrying out the remaining steps.

2. Set oven to 350 degrees Fahrenheit (175 degrees C). In the oven that is getting ready, melt the butter and coat the glass baking dish, which measures 9 x 13 inches. Get rid of the heat.

3. Mix the flour, baking powder, salt, and 3/4 cup of sugar in a bowl. Add milk, just enough to moisten the dry ingredients evenly. Pour uniformly into the baking dish with butter. Spread the batter with the peach and raspberry mixture.

4. Bake for 45 minutes, or until golden brown, in a preheated oven.

32. SANGRIA JELLO SHOTS

PREP TIME 5 MINS

CHILL TIME 3 HRS

TOTAL TIME 3 HRS 5 MINS

INGREDIENTS

- 3 ounces (1 Box) Raspberry Jello
- 1 cup of Boiling Water
- ⅔ cup of Red Wine
- ⅓ cup of Blackberry Brandy
- Fresh Blackberries (non-compulsory)
- Fresh Raspberries (non-compulsory)
- Fresh Strawberries (non-compulsory)
- Fresh Blueberries (non-compulsory)

INSTRUCTIONS

In a medium mixing basin, mix the boiling water and jello; swirl to mix.

1. Brandy and wine are added. Again, stir.
2. Fill every shot glass roughly 3/4 full with an injector or pourable cup of.

3. About three hours should pass before setting up.

4. Slice the strawberries into bits if you want to add some garnish to your jello shots. Add whipped cream and a piece of every fruit to the top of every shot. You may alternatively top the shot with only the fruit and omit the whipped cream entirely. Enjoy!

33. STRAWBERRY CHEESECAKE

prep time: 45 MINUTES

cook time: 1 HOUR 15 MINUTES

resting time: 2 HOURS 20 MINUTES

total time: 4 HOURS 20 MINUTES

Ingredients

- For the crust
- 2 cups of (200 g) graham cracker crumbs, about 2 sleeves
- ¼ cup of (50g) granulated sugar
- 6 tbsp unsalted butter, melted
- For the filling
- 32 ounces (904 g) cream cheese, room temperature
- 1 ⅓ cups of (266 g) granulated sugar
- 1 cup of (227 g) sour cream, room temperature
- 1 tbsp vanilla extract
- ¼ tsp salt
- 4 large eggs, room temperature, lightly beaten
- For the sauce
- 16 ounces (400 g) whole strawberries, diced
- 2 tbsp cornstarch

- 1 cup of (200 g) granulated sugar
- 2 tsp vanilla extract
- ⅛ tsp salt
- 2 cups of (334 g) lightly chop up strawberries

Instructions

1. Build the crust.
2. Set the oven's temperature to 350 degrees Fahrenheit and move the rack to the lowest third. A 9-inch springform pan's exterior bottom should be completely covered in aluminum foil.
3. Mix the sugar, melted butter, and graham cracker crumbs. In the bottom and about two inches up the edges of the pan, press the crumb mixture. For ten minutes, bake. While making the filling, set aside to chill.
4. Creating the filling
5. To 300oF, lower the oven's temperature.
6. Cream cheese should be electric mixer in a large mixing basin until smooth and creamy, about 1 minute.
7. Beat in the sugar and sour cream after adding them. Beat on low speed while adding the vanilla and salt until smooth.
8. Just till mixed, add the eggs with a silicone spatula. Over the prepared crust, pour the batter.
9. Place the cheesecake in the middle of a roasting pan that has been filled with a few inches of boiling water.
10. Bake for an hour, or until the center is just barely jiggly and the sides are golden. After another hour, turn off the oven and leave the cheesecake in the water bath.
11. Place the cheesecake on a wire rack after removing it from the water bath. After removing the cheesecake from the pan with a tiny knife, let it cool for about 1 1/2 hours at room temperature. For at least 4 hours or overnight, cover and chill. Take the pan's sides off. Add the cheesecake to a serving tray after that.
12. Produce the sauce
13. Cornstarch and diced strawberries should be added to a food processor bowl and processed until smooth. Put the sugar in a medium pot after transfer.
14. Cook for about 15 minutes, constantly stirring over medium heat, until thickened.

15. Add the vanilla, salt, and chop up strawberries after taking the pan off the heat. Allow it cool for about 40 minutes while stirring now and again.
16. Just before serving, evenly distribute the topping over the cheesecake or individual slices.

34. STRAWBERRY SORBET

INGREDIENTS

- Yield: Makes 1½ quarts
- 1 whole lemon, seeded and roughly chop up
- 2 cups of sugar
- 2 pounds strawberries, hulled
- Juice of 1 to 2 lemons

PREPARATION

1. Step 1 Mix the sugar and lemon juice in a food processor by pulsing the ingredients. Place in a basin.
2. Step 2 Blend the strawberries in a food processor, then stir them into the lemon juice mixture. If necessary, taste and add extra juice. The strawberries should taste strongly of lemon without being overpowered by it. The mixture should be poured into an ice cream maker and refrigerated.

35. STICKY GINGER CAKE WITH MASCARPONE AND GINGER CREAM RECIPE

Ingredients

- 250g self-raising flour
- 2 tsp ground ginger

- 1 tsp bicarbonate of soda
- 175g (6oz) golden syrup
- 2 tbsp treacle
- 125g (4oz) soft dark brown sugar
- 125g butter
- 3 balls stem ginger, + 2 tbsp syrup (from the jar)
- 2 large eggs
- 250ml milk
- 25g (1oz) crystallised ginger or 1 ball stem ginger, lightly chop up
- For the ginger cream
- 200g (7oz) mascarpone
- 150ml whipping cream
- ½ tsp ground ginger
- 1 stem ginger ball, lightly chop up, + 2 tbsp syrup (from the jar)

Method

1. A 20cm (8in) square cake pan should be greased and lined with nonstick baking paper before the oven is preheated to gas 4, 180°C, and fan 160°C.
2. In a mixing bowl, sift together the flour, ground ginger, baking soda, and 1/4 tsp salt.
3. In a medium saucepan over low heat, mix the golden syrup, treacle, sugar, and butter; whisk until melted. Using a large metal spoon, incorporate the stem ginger mixture into the flour after adding 2 tbsp of the jar's syrup.
4. Mix the milk and eggs in a bowl, then stir in the flour mixture. Spread the crystallized or stem ginger over the top of the mixture and spoon it into the prepared baking dish. Bake for 35 minutes, or until a skewer inserted in the center comes out clean. In the tin, cool.
5. WATCH: How should a skewer be kept in good condition?
6. Play Movie
7. Mascarpone has to be whisked until soft peaks form for the ginger cream. Whip the cream and incorporate it, along with the ground ginger, stem ginger, and syrup, into the mascarpone. Slice the cake into 16 squares, then serve every one warm with a dollop of ginger cream on the side.

36. SWEET POTATO CRÈME BRÛLÉE

Prep30 Min

Total9 Hr 35 Min

Servings10

Ingredients

- 1large sweet potato, baked, peel off and mashed (1 1/4 cups of)
- 1/4cup of packed light brown sugar
- 1tbsp fresh lemon juice
- 2cups of whipping cream
- 3/4cup of granulated sugar
- 7egg yolks, slightly beaten
- 3tsp vanilla
- 1/3cup of packed light brown sugar

Steps

1. 1
2. 325°F oven temperature. 10 inch quiche plate, with butter. Lemon juice, 1/4 cup of brown sugar, and mashed sweet potatoes should all be mixd in a medium basin. Pour the ingredients into a quiche pan.
3. 2
4. Mix whipping cream, granulated sugar, egg yolks, and vanilla in a 2-quart saucepan. Cook for about 15 minutes, stirring often, over medium-low heat (do not boil). Give the sweet potato mixture a pour. Put the dish in the pan. Put a pan in the oven. Pour 3/4 inch of boiling water or more into the pan (about halfway up side of dish).
5. 3

6. Bake for one hour, or until center of knife inserted almost comes out clean. Remove the dish from the water with care. On a cooling rack, cool. Cover and chill for at least eight hours.

7. 4

8. Set the broil setting on the oven. Place custard in a 15x10x1-inch pan and sprinkle with 1/3 cup of brown sugar. For 3 to 5 minutes, or until sugar is melted, broil with the top 4 to 6 inches from the flame. Before serving, let stand for five minutes.

37. TIRAMISU

Prep Time: 30 mins

Cook Time: 5 mins

Additional Time: 5 hrs

Total Time: 5 hrs 35 mins

Servings: 12

Ingredients

- 6 large egg yolks
- ¾ cup of white sugar
- ⅔ cup of milk
- 1 ¼ cups of heavy cream
- ½ tsp vanilla extract
- 1 pound mascarpone cheese, at room temperature
- ¼ cup of strong brewed coffee, at room temperature
- 2 tbsp rum
- 2 (3 ounce) packages ladyfinger cookies
- 1 tbsp unsweetened cocoa powder

Directions

1. In a medium saucepan, mix sugar and egg yolks and stir until completely mixd. Over medium heat, whisk in the milk and stir continuously until the mixture boils.

2. Gently boil for 1 minute, then turn off the heat and let the food cool slightly.

3. Refrigerate for one hour with a tightly sealed cover.

4. In a medium bowl, use an electric mixer to beat the cream and vanilla until stiff peaks form.

5. Take the egg yolk mixture out of the fridge, whisk in the mascarpone cheese, and serve.

6. In a small bowl, mix the coffee and rum. Ladyfingers should be slice in half lengthwise and drizzled with the coffee concoction.

7. Half of the soaked ladyfingers should be arranged in the bottom of a 7 x 11-inch dish. The ladyfingers should be covered with half of the mascarpone mixture, followed by half of the whipped cream. Apply layers one more time. Cocoa powder should be added on top.

8. Cover and chill for 4 to 6 hours, or until set.

Made in United States
Troutdale, OR
04/14/2025